The
WEALTH
TRANSFER
Agenda

DR. D. K. OLUKOYA

Warfare Prayer Series 5

The Wealth Transfer Agenda

DR. D. K. OLUKOYA

D. K. OLUKOYA

THE WEALTH TRANSFER AGENDA
© 2005 DR. D. K. OLUKOYA
ISBN 978-0692231852
1st Printing · May 2005 AD

Published by:
The Battle Cry Christian Ministries
322, Herbert Macaulay Way, Yaba, P. O. Box 12272, Ikeja. Lagos.
website: www.battlecrychristianministries.org
email: info@battlecrychristianministries.org
Phone: 0803-304-4239, 0803-306-0073

All Scripture quotations are from the King James Version of the Bible

THE WEALTH TRANSFER AGENDA

God has an agenda for the end time. It is an agenda which will amaze both believers and unbelievers alike. In the real sense, wealth belongs to God and He gives it to whosoever He wills.

Wealth or riches occupy an important place in God's end-time programme for the world. Unknown to most believers, wealth is not just needed for personal survival; God needs wealth for the execution of the divine programme. For example, the preaching of the gospel cannot be successfully carried out without money.

THE AGENDA

God has a secret agenda, which will k eep the entir e population of the world gaping in wonder. W hat is this secret agenda? We are living in an age where the real wonders of the gospel ar e going to b e unfolded. We have seen a little of that phenomenon in the past twenty years.

There was a time several years ago, when gathering a hundred thousand crowds together seemed impossible. Again, several years ago, nobody wo uld have thought o f a large ga thering w here t wo millio n people would gather to gether to pray and listen to God's word. Now, su ch ma mmoth cro wds are becoming regular occurrences in t he hist ory o f Pentecostal Christianity.

Explosive church growth, unprecedented records of conversionand church attendance are clear indications of the fact that we are in the thre shold of the wonders of the end-time. In this season and the years ahead, individual Christians and churches should brace up to witness such wonders as would amaze all a nd sundry.

FINANCIAL EMPOWERMENT

To fully accomplish and execute God's goals   for the end times, individuals a nd churches will receive amazing financial empowerment. Tow ards this end, the Church of God will very so on become the controller of the economy of the world. God who   is the author of wealth, will ens ure that abundant wealth is channelled towards where real action is taking place – the church.

If a church was blessed with thousands, Go d would move her to the le vel of millions, just to enable her maximally   execute t he divine project of world evangelization. Again, if a church has access to millions, God will move her toa level w here there is access to billions. As God rounds off His programme of evangelization and global revival, churches that are at the cutting e dge of the end-time revival are going to wax stronger and stronger globally.

Of what use is wealth if it is not channelled towards the preaching of the gospel? If there are lots of idle funds lying here and there in man y parts of the world, of what use are such funds if they are not expended on the preaching of the gospel?

We are living in a crucial time as far as God's end time agenda is concerned. So meone has aptly described the time in whic h we are living as injury time.

There is no time to waste. The situation in the world is too frightening and alarming. In South Africa, one thousand people are buri ed daily as a result of AIDS. The global suicide rate has reached an a ll-time high. One suicide takes place every forty seconds a nd one million people commit suicide every year. It is on record that 12 million African children have been made orphans by AID S. According to W HO, so me four hundred and fifty million of the worlds 6.4 billion people suffer mental related problems.

THE RESCUE PLAN

God cannot fold his arms and watch the people whom He created perish. He has fashioned an emergency rescue plan just before the end of the world. The devil has changed gear because he knows that he has a short time.

Rev. 12:12: Therefore rejoice, ye heavens, and ye that dwell in them. Woe to the inhabiters of the earth and of the sea! for the devil is come down unto you , having great wrath, because he knoweth that he hath but a short time.

Much as the devil can come up with emergency plans to destroy millions of people all over the world, God has also come up with the plan for the massive conversion of souls. For this plan to be effectively executed, so much money will be required. No wonder the Bible says;

Zech. 1:17: Cry yet, saying, Thus saith the Lord of hosts; My cities through prosperity shall yet be spread abroad; and the Lord shall yet comfort Zion, and shall yet choose Jerusalem.

This is the hour when the passage above will be actualized. This is the time when more money than has ever been made available for the preaching of the gospel will be released unto the church. God is going to raise up individuals and churches as end-time treasurers. This is the essence of the mystery of the wealth transfer agenda.

God is going to bless His people in unimaginable ways; with stupendous wealth. It will be carried out in a process called 'Wealth Transfer'. Beside the global need of the gospel, God's prosperity plan f or each of His children is another reason why we all need to understand the mystery of the transfer of wealth.

THE REVELATION

Whichever way we look at it, we all need sound knowledge concerning God's plan and programme towards the financial empowerment of His children. Ignorance will keep the poor perpetually poor while knowledge will effect a change of status. What you know concerning God's programme will become a springboard towards aspiring for and attaining the next level in life.

Ignorance has caused enough damage among God's people, gross ignorance has made princes to trek while servants are riding on horses. This aberration has continued unabated for a very l ong time.

Since, the gentiles have captu red the wealth meant for God's people, God is set toreverse the situation. He cannot sit in heaven and watch this ugly trend continue. God is going to make such sweeping changes, that will baffle the entire world. The Gentiles are going to become poorer while the believers will get richer. The manner with which God will do this will remain an enigma.

At the end of the day, it is going to become clear that the power to get wealth comes from God alone and it is given to whosoever He chooses. This book will, therefore, open your eyes to behold God's end-time programme as well as position you strategically. In all, you should never let this great opportunity slip off your fingers. You must grasp this golden opportunity and allow God to have His way in your life.

UNDERSTANDING THE AGENDA

What then is the essence of the wealth transfer agenda? It is a programme whereby, God enriches individuals or churches financially. This programme has already started. It is my prayer that nobody will be left out in this great move of God.

Let us examine a passage of the Bible through which we shall gain great insights into God's end-time programme.

Proverbs 13:22: A good man leaveth an inheritance to his children's children: and the wealth of the sinner is laid up for the just.

There is an amazing revelation in that passage. The Bible tells us that the wealth of sinners is laid down for the just. Here, we discover that there is going to be a remarkable transfer of wealth from the camp of the gentiles to that of the saints.

Let us examine another passage.

Job 27:13-15: This is the portion of a wicked man with God, and the heritage of oppressors, which they shall receive of the Almighty. If his children be multiplied, it is for the sword: and his offspring shall not be satisfied with bread. Those that remain of him shall be buried in death: and his widows shall not weep.

These are the words of the AlmightyGod. If you are familiar with the word of God you would have discovered that God does not joke with His words. Remember, heaven and earth may pass away but God's word will never pass away.

The above passage reiterates the fact of wealth transfer. As it is characteristic of every declaration from God, every word written above shall come to pass.

God has a wealth transfer agenda, which will be fulfilled to the latter. God shall personally instruct, supervise and effect a transfer of the wealth of the Gentile s into the coffers of His children. We therefore, need to be prep ared to witness and experience this divine agenda.

SLAVING FOR THE RIGHTEOUS

As if what God has said is not enough, t he Bible goes on to unfold another aspect of the wealth transfer agenda.

Eccles. 2:26: For God giveth to a man that is good in his sight wisdom, and knowledge, and joy: but to the sinne r he giveth travail, to gather and to heap up, that he may give to him that is good before God. This also is vanity and vexation of spirit.

The Bible tells us, here, that a sinner may be allowed to labour and amass wealth only for such wealth to b e transferred to the righteous. Do you wonder how God does this? You shall soon discover His method in this book.

This topic is so serious that one of the respected prophets in the Bible made deep declarations concerning it.

Isaiah 61:5-6: And strangers shall stand and feed your flocks, and the sons of the alien shall be your plow men and your vinedressers. But ye shall be named the Priests of the Lord: men shall call you the Ministers of our God: ye shall eat the riches of the Gentiles, and in their glory shall ye boast yourselves.

Here, Isaiah the Messianic prophet, unfolds the mystery of wealth transfer. Do you know that wealth is not only acquired through handwork? A good proportion of wealth is divinely transferred. When God makes you a beneficiary of wealth transfer, people around you will never understand how you managed to acquire such unprecedented wealth.

WEALTH BELONGS TO GOD

God has designed to make you reap the riches of the Gentiles. If your mind has been startled by the passages we have read so far, let us read one more passage and you will discover that God means business as far as the wealth transfer agenda is concerned.

Haggai 2:8: The silver is mine, and the gold is mine, saith the Lord of hosts.

What we discover here is that, the totality of silver and gold in the world actuall y be longs to God and that the onus of transferring it f rom one person to anot her or from one place to anothe r rests squarely on God's shoulders. Therefore, God can decide to transfer wealth or riches in such a manner, as to empower His children to carry out their divine assignments, by undertaking such programmes and projects t hat will lead to the expansion of God's kingdom here on earth.

RECOVERING THE LOST WEALTH

You may wonder, "why all these emphases on wealth transfer? Why do we need divine enlightenment or information concerning wealth transfer? It is simply because of the re aso n expatiated below.

To recover your ancestors' lostwealth. Has it ever dawned on you that majority of the people whoever lived since creation, have had no access whatsoever to the amount of wealth with which they were endowed with by God? The situation is worse in Africa as most of our ancestors lived and died poor.

INCALCULABLE LOSS

Most people have lived and died struggling below poverty line. Such lost wealth can be recovered today even now that our ancestors have died. If some of us can just recover a fraction of what our ancestors lost, such persons would have recovered enough resources to feed the entire nation.

Many of our forefathers died as paupers when they were divinely destined to be extremely rich. They lived and died poor because they were serving ragged familiar spirits. Idol worship made them to be poor when they were supposed to have the type of riches which would have remained a record in history till date.

Many of them, besides serving idols, formed covenants with evil spirits that th ey we re going to be poor. Some of the idols, which they served, required them to make a vow of poverty. Hence, they lost so much riches.

Through idolatry, many of our ancestors buried their wealth and indeed, that of their offsprings. If they had been rich, generations of children would have benefited from such rich inheritance. It is through a book like 'Wealth Transfer Agenda' that such lost wealth can be reco vered.

Let me share a true-life experience with you. Several years ago, a particular brother had a strange experience. This brother sat for G.C.E. examination and made seven straight As. He sat for advanced level G.C.E. and made three As. By the time he travelled abroad, he bagged first class honours. He then came to Nigeria hoping to find a good job.

In those days, findin g a good job after schooling was quite easy. In fact, in those days, graduating stu dents were offered jobs w hile writ ing their final examinations. In other words, employment was guaranteed. Also, immediately graduates got jobs, they were offered cars and good accommodation.

In strange circumstances, this man with a first class

degree in Economics, trudged the streets for two years without securing any employment. He was brilliant, well trained and qualified and yet nobody was prepared to offer him a job. Wherever he found advertisements concerning job offers, he was turned down inspite of the fact that he was qualified. Even those who had third class degrees were offered jobs.

The young man did not even get a job he could manage. As he continued roaming the streets, his eyes one day, caught the banner of a crusade. Since he was unemployed, he made up his mind to attend. Before he attended the crusade, he was only familiar with Orthodox Christianity. He was attending a church where his pastor would read the entire sermon from a notebook. He was therefore surprised, when he discovered that the preacher at the crusade did not read from any notebook.

The preacher preached on the 'fourth man in the fire' and emphasized how the same fourth man can bring out anyone who happens to be grappling with the intense heat of unbearable fire.

The unemployed graduate listened attentively. The

fact that the preacher was describing a problem which sounded like his fascinated him. He saw in the preacher's illustration an exact replica of what he was going through. The young man did not hesitate to give his life to Christ at the instance of an altar call.

God took him into a trance where he made an amazing discovery. While he was busy crying and praying, God opened his eyes. He saw an angel dressed in white and he decided to find out what was happening. The angel declared, "I am an angel of the living God, follow me and I will show you the secrets of your problems." In that brief trance the angel led him to the graveyard and took him to a particular person's grave.

The angel struck the grave and shouted with a loud voice, "Victoria, come out." To the surprise of the unemployed graduate, a woman came out of the grave. The angel went ahead and ordered the woman, "return what you have stolen from this young man." The woman who came out of the grave was frightened and confused saying "I'm sorry, I can no longer figure out where I buried it." The angel insisted that the grave woman must do ev erything to fetch the items stolen from the young man.

The woman bent down and started digging the ground. After a long while, she brought out an it em which had the resemblance of a wedding pr esent. From the appearance of the item it must have been buried for quite a long time. The angel ordered the woman to retur n the item back to t he graduat e. He stretched forth his hand and collected it.

Being a very brilliant man, he decided to ask questions.

"Please, y ou have int roduced y ourself as an a ngel, can you tell me something about the identity of this woman?"

"That is your grandmother," replied the angel.

Puzzled, the young man continued, "but I never knew her, she died before I was born."

The brother asked further, "w hat ex actly did she hand over to me?"

"It is your virtue", the angel replied.

"How manage? How could she have done that when she died before I was born?" The brother asked again.

The angel gave him a clue, "Your grandmother was still alive when you were in the womb. She carried out the evil operation before you were born. Precisely, the deed was done when you were exactly six months in the womb. She stole your virtue and buried it at that time. That is what you have just collected."

By the time the angel made his last statement, the preacher at the crusade was rounding off with "In Jesus' name we pray. Amen."

It was a never-to-be-forgotten-experience for the young man. He had never seen such a revelation before. However, he knew that he had had an encounter with God. The crusade was brought to an end and he went back home. He got up the following day and decided to continue his usual search for a job. Ten minutes after he started trekking in search of job, he heard a car screech to a halt and he sighted a good-looking executive coming out of an expensive car and flashing a smile at him. He took a second look at the young man and discovered that it was his erstwhile schoolmate. He discovered to his surprise that his schoolmate who was more or less a numbskull had now made it.

In those days, h e used to teach this fellow lots o f subjects including mathematics. The devil is indeed, very wicked. He made a g enius jobless whi le a total dullard was gainfully employed a nd living comfortably.

The man who came out of the car was surprised to see his former classmate trekking.

"Where have you been over the years"? He asked.

The joble ss youn g man narrated how he had been jobless inspite of his brilliant academic c areer. H is well-to-do friend managed to listen to his s tory for a while and told him to come into the car. The unemployed man's friend o ffered to take him t o the General Manager of the company where he worked.

As soon as they got there, he said, "General Manager, meet the person who was teaching me mathematics and made me to get pass marks fro m the background of scoring zeroes in mathematics. He needs a j ob. Kindly offer him an employment."

When the unemployed graduate tendered his certificates, the General M anager opened his mouth wide. He could not imagine how someone with su ch a brilliant academic record could have remained jobless for two years and so cleared his thr oat and said; "I am going to give youa job right away. Name the type of car you want the company to giv e you, name your salary, too. Tell me the type of accommodation you l ike and the part of the city you want to live in."

The unemployed graduate was dazed. However, h e tabled his requirements and that was how he was given a job, a brand-new car, a posh apartment and a fantastic salary. The day after his enco unter with the angel, he experienced a miraculous turn around breakthroughs simply because, he recovered his stolen virtue through prayer. He would have remained jobless inspite of his academic excellence.

THE REWIND FUNCTION

A lot of people are going back and forth on the streets without any employment today because their virtues have been stolen. You must pray for the recovery of your stolen virtue today. Moreover, you must also recover the stolen wealth ofyour ancestors. You can pray that such wealth should be accumulated and handed to you.

In the spiritual realm there is a facility for reverse. You can do a spiritual rewind into a hundred years of your ancestors past and recover the totality of the wealth which was stolen.

Anything is possible in the spiritual realm. When you achieve the recovery of a huge wealth or resources stolen from your ancestors, people around you will be amazed at the amount of wealth which you will acquire through such a simple practice.

Many of us are languishing in poverty today because, our wealth, as well as that of our ancestors, have been stolen. Great prosperity will be received and acquired when you take this simple step.

At this point I want you to pray the following prayer points:

Every virtue of my life, buried by household wickedness, come out by fire, in the name of Jesus.

I command every virtue and wealth stolen from my ancestors to be released unto me now, in the name of Jesus.

THE BLUE PRINT

God has waited for so long to see His beloved children discover His plan and purpose concerning wealth transfer. God desires to change the economic situation of His children through wealth transfer. In this chapter we shall examine, in specific terms, certain details concerning the divine plan.

By the time you are thoroughly informed of God's intention and plan to effect a transfer of huge financial resources into your account, you will rise up, possess your possessions and say bye-bye to poverty.

Let us examine the details of the wealth transfer agenda.

☞ To Withdraw And Pocket The Wealth Of The Ungodly

God has designed that the sinner should work very hard and accumulate wealth only to transfer it to the righteous. When the ungodly begins to labour, they do so with the intention of enriching themselves. By the time they begin to stockpile their wealth, God will spring a surprise and order them to channel their gains to the storehouse of the righteous.

God's plan and intention is to make the unrighteous be slaves to the righteous. This is an integral part of the divine wealth transfer agenda.

☞ To Reap Where Unbelievers Have Laboured

This may appear very strange to modern day Christians. By and large, believers have drawn a line of demarcation between the wealth of a sinner and that of the righteous. So, when God begins to make a believer reap the proceeds of the unbeliever's labour, there are certain reactions. This is due to ignorance. There is nothing wrong in reaping what the ungodly spent time to labour for. It is only one of the metho ds through which God will execute His divine wealth transfer policy.

Sometimes, the ways of God may baffle even the most enlightened believer. The Bible has made it clear. The principles of the kingdom may often sound strange. No matter how strange kingdom's principles are, you must be simple enough to understand and accept God's methods of blessing the righteous.

Romans 11:33: O the depth of the riches both of the wisdom and knowledge of God! how unsearchable are his judgments, and his ways past finding out!

When the Bible declares that something is past finding out, it is simply referring to a mystery. If you can catch a glimpse of what this principle is all about you will be amazed at what God will begin to do in your life. This is exactly what Jesus meant when he declared:

John 4:38: I sent you to reap that whereon ye bestowed no labour: other men laboured, and ye are entered into their labours.

The economy of heaven operates in a very different manner. The people of the world may tell you that you must work your fingers to the bone, get involved in sharp practices and adopt the get-rich-quick principle, if need be. God's method is different.

As far as God is concerned, He will allow the unbeliever to labour and when they are about reaping the benefits of their labour, He beckons on one of His children saying: "Get up, go there and reap what that fellow spent time and energy sowing." This is the mystery of wealth transfer.

How does this happen? An unbeliever sets up a company, invests huge amount in establishing it and dies prematurely. Then in a moment God raises up one of the managers who happens to be a believer and he becomes Chairman and Managing Director of the company. Within a few years, the believer may become the owner of the company while the family of the former owner, will in certain mysterious circumstances begin to depend on what the believer gives them for sustenance.

One of these days, lots of Chairmen and Managing Directors of some companies will retire or give way for children of God to take over. When this happens, it is God at work.

THE WEALTH TRANSFER AGENDA

God is executing His wealth transfer agenda. Of course, God has a reason for doing this. He knows that the children of the devil cannot glorify Him or sponsor the preaching of the gospel with their wealth. That is why He programmed things in a way as to make the righteous inherit the wealth of the unrighteous.

In any case, the wealth which the unbelievers struggle to accumulate belongs to God.

Psalm 50:10: For every beast of the forest is mine, and the cattle upon a thousand hills.

Silver and gold belong to God. Therefore, no unbeliever has any right to lay claim to any wealth acquired legally or stolen. Even where wealth is acquired through proper channel, it is still a gift from God. The Bible says:

1 Cor. 4:7: For who maketh thee to differ from another? and what hast thou that thou didst not receive? now if thou didst receive it, why dost thou glory, as if thou hadst not received it?

If God has given unbelievers access to wealth, He can also decide to channel the same wealth to a place which will be most useful to Him and His kingdom.

We need a renewed mind set on the subject of wealth transfer.

☞ To Acquire Silver and Gold stored Up By the Unrighteous

If you have been studying business trends in the world, you would have discovered that, it is characteristic of unbelievers to store more than they will ever require. This habit of amassing wealth does not glorify God. It can only boost the ego of the rich.

If you take a look at the manner, with which the rich store the money which they may not need, it will amaze you. There are some Africans living or dead, who have enough money to finance the economy of some nations in the continent for a period of ten years. Some of these extremely rich Africans (living or dead) can sponsor one hundred churches or ministries between now and the time the rapture will take place. Such idle funds are being stacked away in foreign accounts.

Hundred years from now, if the Lord tarries, there will be idle funds in excess of millions of dollars in some dormant foreign accounts. This is the time for us to begin to pray that God will b egin to transfer, the stocked up wealth or piled up wealth of the rich to faithful believers. In fact, this should form an essential part of your daily prayer points.

So much finances and resources are lying idle in form of reserves. These reserves are needed by believers who are burdened for evangelism, church planting and the establishment of the saints.

☞ To Receive Multiple Promotion

If there is anyone who needs promotion, it is the righteous. There are believers who have not experienced any form of promotion within ten o r twenty years. Some have not received a single promotion, not to talk of double promotion. Do you also know that God can give you triple promotion? Promotion comes from God. The Bible says:

Psalm 75:6: For promotion cometh neither from the east, nor from the west, nor from the south.

When God wants to transfer wealth into the account of the righteous, He grants a believer double, triple or more promotions. This kind of promotion is a reflection of God's intention to give the believer financial empowerment.

God is so much in a hurry to accomplish the task of world evangelization within a short time that He will stop at nothing to promote His children. Here, I have a word for believers who have experienced this kind of promotion. God has granted you uncommon financial promotionbecause He wants you to invest part of what you now have in the work of the kingdom.

Of what use are the millions that are lying idle in various accounts at home and abroad? Why not channel some of those idle funds towards printing of tracts, opening of new branches, supporting missionaries and taking the gospel far and wide?

Honestly, I am waiting for the time when those who have received extraordinary blessings from God will raise cheques, that will match the level of blessings which God has given to them. If a man who had been blessed with several millions manages to give a few thousands to the church, such a person is living in ignorance as far as wealth transfer agenda is concerned.

The Bible says:

Luke 12: 48: But he that knew not, and did commit things worthy of stripes, shall be beaten with few stripes.' For unto whomsoever much is given, of him shall be much required: and to whom men have committed much, of him they will ask the more.

☞ To Take Back Seven-Fold Wha The Enemy Has Stolen

The enemy has stolen lots of virtues and blessings from the hands of many of the children of God. Such stolen virtues must be recovered.

The issue of wealth transfer can only be understood when we understand certain Biblical principles. In Bible days, whenever a thief was caught, he was instructed to restore seven-fold what he stole. If your wealth or that of your ancestors was ever stolen at any time, you must seek reparation. In other words, you must insist that all stolen things be recovered.

However, since the Bible says that the thief must restore seven-fold, you will need to demand that your stolen wealth be restored seven-fold.

It is unfort unate however, that many of us have not obtained the principal, not to talk about obtaining seven-fold our stolen wealth. This is true about a number of God's children. Many are living in abject poverty because they know little or nothing concerning the principles of the Scriptures. When the devil knows that you know your rights in the gospel, he will release to you, what belongs to you. He will also comply, when you order him or his agents to return seven-fold.

The problem is that many believers go through life without praying about stolen blessings. W hy would God command the thief to restore seven-fold? I t is because He knows that certain departments in the realm of the spirit are involved in the thefts of virtues and blessings. The moment you begin to pray, you will experience the recovery and the devil will be forced to pay interests on what he has stolen.

Don't forget the three principles which stand out from the above passage. One, the thief must be caught. The Bible says, if a thief be not caught, you cannot recover what is stolen if you are not able to catch the thief. So, you m ust fi rst catch the th ief before you begin the mission of recovery.

The second thing you must do, is to order the thief to return what he stole. You will find appropriate prayer points at the end of t his book to help in t his area.

The third thing you must do, is to follow the Scriptural principles of making the thief go the extra mile of restoring seven-fold.

God has given the believer, the power of attorney to execute vengeance upon the ungodly.

Psalm 149:4-9: For the Lord taketh pleasure in his people: he will beautify the meek with salvation. Let the saints be joyful in glory: let them sing aloud upon their beds. Let the high praises of God be in their mouth, and a twoedged sword in their hand; To execute vengeance upon the heathen, and punishments upon the people; To bi nd their kings with chains, and their nobles with fetters of iron; To execute upon them the judgment w ritten: th is honour have all his saints. Praise ye the Lord.

THE REALITY OF GOD'S AGENDA

You must get to a point in life where you begin to interpret earthly realities in the light of spiritual principles.

The level of wealth acquired by any individual, is bye and large, the product of certain principles. If wealth were to be acquired only by hard work and being connected to those who are rich, some of us may never know anything called riches.

I was raised in humble beginnings. My parents were not well-off by any standard. When I was young, I struggled with poverty. In those days, I had just one kettle; with the kettle I would cook my rice, scoop it out and use the same kettle to cook the stew. If wealth were to be acquired through one's background, I would have remained a poor man today.

I would not have come anywhere near obtaining a doctorate degree if not for the good fortunes of a scholarship. Then, I was a boy who struggled with poverty, studying in England, sitting side by side with the children of extremely rich Africans. I had access to the best of academic opportunities not because I inherited wealth, but because God was offering me such golden opportunities on the platter of what I now know to be wealth transfer.

How else could someone from a poor background have been given free access to excellent educational facilities to the point of making a first class and attaining doctoral level in flying colours? Now, I understand better.

But for wealth transfer, generations of several families would have forever remained poor, uneducated and backward. The mystery of wealth transfer would remain the only hope for those who are raised from poor background. You shall understand what I mean as you read on.

According to secular views, the poor are supposed to get poorer while the rich become richer. The good news however, is that, spiritual principles supercede physical principles. God can decide to make any of His children enjoy the wealth of the Gentiles and grant access to what is meant exclusively for the rich and their offsprings. The mystery of wealth transfer explains it all.

Here, we shall examine certain methods or means through which God transfers the wealth of the ungodly to the righteous.

☞ **To Win Scholarship from Distant or Foreign Land**

Divine wealth transfer takes place when scholarships are won. I happen to be a beneficiary of this agenda. I won a scholarship to do a doctoral programme. My father could not afford the air ticket then, not to talk about the school fees.

There are lots of believers who n eed to key-in to the anointing of receiving foreign and local scholarships. It is God's plan to ma ke believers study in the best schools abroad at the e xpense of some individuals or the government of some nations.

The Bible says;

Isaiah 49:23: And kings shall be thy nursi ng fathers, and their queens thy nursing mothers: they shall bow dow n to thee with their face toward the earth, and l ick up the dust of thy feet; and thou shalt know that I a m the Lord: for they shall not be ashamed that wait for me.

You can pray the anointing of sp onsorship upon your children when you cannot afford such huge expenses. As a Christian parent, your ch ildren can make use of money which does not belo ng to you and get the best type of education available.

☞ To buy off materials acquiredby the ungodly

This is one of the media of wealt h tra nsfer. There are many things the children of God may not be able to acquire without wealth transfer. Most of these items are priced abo ve the level of Christian believers who are not able to make ends meet. Go d can make the wealthy buy some gadgets, equipments, properties or cars at a very high price and sell it to you cheaply.

☞ **To develop your busine ss to the level where it will swallow other ungodly business ventures**

Have you ever witnessed a s ituation whe re unbelievers mysteriously clo se up their shops while the business of a believer continues to boom?

Let me share a testimony with you. We held a business breakthrough programme som e years ago. There was a particular sister who experienced an amazing transfer of wealth. Before God bless ed he r in an extraordinary ma nner, s he actually suf fered. She struggled with poverty and her means of sustenance was selling cooked rice and stew to primary school pupils.

Whenever the pupils go on break, they rushed to the stall of the food sellers. The sister discovered that the young pupils would flock to the stall of other rice sellers and abandon her own stall. At the close of business each day she would go back home with a large bowl of cooked rice and stew which she could not sell. Her children always complaine d tha t they had more than enough rice to eat at home. The mother never explained to them that she b rought the surplus rice home as a result of the misfortune of inability to sell. That was how she continued in frustration to cook rice and stew which no pupil was willing to buy .

God came to her rescue when we held a wealth transfer prayer meeting at the inception of the ministry. There the Lord visited her. Power changed hands and the wealth of her unbelieving competitors was transferred miraculously to her.

After the programme, by the tim e s he went back to her business, the tide had turned and the sist er's stall had become a be ehive of activiti es. It was a s if the pupils held a meeting and decided to buy their food from no other person but the sister. Whatever amount of rice the si ster took to the school, finished in record time. Surprisingly, her contemporaries were no longer selling. At the close of business, they all carried cooked rice they could not sell home.

When the trend continued, all t he other rice sellers

packed up. The only person selling rice was the Christian sister. Of cour se, she knew that what was happening was a product of a spiritual transfer of wealth. The sister discovered that a believer's business can indeed, swallow the businesses of others. The sister's business swallowed up those of others.

If at the moment the enemy happens to have fired arrows at your business, God will interv ene by dealing decisively with the e nemy. God will do a new thing in your life. He will channel to you, the wealth of the heathens.

HISTORY OF WEALTH TRANSFER

So far, we have discovered that the wealth transfer agenda is one crucial factor which will introduce breath-taking changes into the lives of believers in this generation. It is crystal clear that it is the will of God to give us the riches of the Gentiles. God expects His children to take charge of the wealth of the nations. It has become clear that sinners are just accumulating their wealth, waiting for us t o take over. Before now, the devil and his children have captured the wealth of the world. The devil started out with an intentionor goal; to con trol the world by controlling its wealth.

On the top of the list in God's agend a is a plan to move wealth from the camp of the unrighteous to the camp of t he saints. Di versions of wealth is one act of God which can be very interesting to witness. When God diverts wealth fro m the camp of the wicked to the camp of t he righteous, God's people may exhibit some reluctance, if there is lack of understanding in the area of principles of wealth transfer.

A SCRIPTURAL PHENOMENON

Right from Bible days, God had started this transfer. As God brings His agenda for the world to a clo se, we are going to witness the most massive transfer in the history of the world. As we get ready to witness this, let us examine instances of such transfers in the Scripture.

☞ **Wealth Transfer As Experienced By A braham**

God had a unique plan in which Abraham was to play a crucial role. Abraham became intimately related to God. There was no way God's plan for Abraham could have been fulfilled if he had remained poor.

God factored a wealth transfer agenda to make Abraham occupy the right place in His divine programme. The covenant which the Lord had with Abraham did not only bring blessings into his life, it made him inherit the riches of the Gentiles. From nowhere Abraham suddenly became rich.

Genesis 13:2 : And Abram was very rich in cattle, in silver, and in gold.

Abraham, therefore, became a refer ence point as far as riches are concerned.

☞ Wealth Transfer As Experienced By Joseph

God had a plan in which Joseph was to play a prominent role. Although a lot of people were rich in his time, but when he came on the scene, he became exceptionally rich. The wealth of the world resided in Egypt but God had to move Joseph from the land of his nativity into the land of Egypt. God had to trouble Pharaoh with a dream which became an av enue for wealth transfer.

From the pit to prison and from the pris on to the

palace, Joseph became the only one who was the sole administrator of the richest nation at that time. Pharaoh was only a ceremonial leader.

Genesis 41:41: And Pharaoh said unto Joseph, See, I have set thee over all the land of Egypt.

The implication of becoming the Prime Minister of Egypt was that by that appointment, Joseph was sitting on a gold mine. Joseph did not only occupy the position of a Prime Minister, his purse was affected. He became rich.

Genesis 41:52: And the name of the second called he Ephraim:For God hath caused me to be f ruitful in the land of my affliction.

His personal declaration was that God has made him fruitful. The wealth of Egypt was transferred to him. One major function of Joseph as Prime Minister was to sell corn. Thus, he became the sole controller of the wealth of Egypt. The Bible tells us that all coun tries of the world came to Joseph to buy food.

Genesis 41:57: And all countries came into Egypt to Joseph for to buy corn; because that thefamine was so sore in all lands.

To understand the meaning of what we have just read let us take a look into how Joseph controlled Egypt's wealth.

Genesis 42:25: Then Joseph commanded to fill their sacks with corn, and to restore every man's money into his sack, and to give them provision for the way: and thus did he unto them.

Joseph had the power to give food free of charge to his brethren. Moreover, by virtue of his office, he could give out money without being questioned. Joseph was not a native of Egypt. If you have discovered wealth transfer in Joseph's life in what you have read so far, you have not seen anything yet.

A time came when Joseph had absolute power to control the economy of the whole world.

Genesis 47:13-15: And there was no bread in all the land; for the famine was very sore, so that the land of Egypt and all the land of Canaan fainted by reason of the famine. And Joseph gathered up all the money that was found in the land of Egypt, and in the land of Canaan, for the corn which they bought: and Joseph brought the money into Pharaoh's house. And when money failed in the land of Egypt, and in the land of Canaan, all the Egyptians came unto Joseph, and said, Give us bread: for why should we die in thy presence? for the money faileth.

In the then whole world , there was only one man under whose control was the world economy; Joseph. God so endowed him with wisdom to the point he bought off all their lands and cattle.

Genesis 47:16, 17, 20: And Joseph said. Give your cattle; and I will give you for your cattle, if money fail. . . . And they brought their cattle unto Jos eph: and Joseph gave them bread in exchange for horses, and for the flocks, and for the cattle of the herds, and for the asses: and he fed them with bread for all their cattle for that year. . . . A nd Joseph bought all the land of Egypt for Pharaoh; for the Egyptians sold every man his field, because the famine prevailed over them: so the land became Pharaoh's.

Funny enough, people offered themselves to Joseph to be bought in exchange f or food.

Genesis 47:18-19: When that year was ended, they came unto him the second year, and said unto him. We will not hide it from my lord, how that our money is spent; my lord also hath our herds of cattle; there is not ought l eft in the sight of my lord, but our bodies, and our lands: Wherefore shall we die before thine eyes, both we and our land? buy us and our land for bread, and we and our land will b e servants unto

Pharaoh : and give us seed, that we may live, and not die, tha t the land be not desolate.

This is a classical example of wealth transfer. One of these days, unbelievers will bring their equipments, cars and landed properties begging you to purchase them for a ridiculous amount. When such things happen, it is God giving you the miracle of wealth transfer.

To crown the wealth transfer, Joseph and his family became stupendously rich even in a strange land.

Genesis 47:27: And Israel dwelt in the land of Egypt, in the country of Goshen; and they had possessions therein, and grew, and multiplied exceedingly.

Thus, Israel took possession and exercised control over the wealth of Egypt.

☞ Wealth Transfer And Daniel

Daniel was one of the Hebrew children who found themselves in a strange land. Nebuchadnezzar the king of Babylon carried out an invasion which resulted in Daniel, Shedrack, Meshack and Abednego being taken captive. As far as wealth was concerned Babylon dominated the scene in that era.

Again God had to allow his children to go from slavery to dominion prosperity. Although Nebuchadnezzar was stupendously rich, God brought Daniel into prominence and transferred the wealth into his coffers.

Daniel 2:48: Then the king made Daniel a great man, and gave him many great gifts, and made him ruler over the whole province of Babylon, and chief of the governors over all the wise men of Babylon.

Daniel and Joseph had something in common. In this case Daniel was not only a Prime Minister, when Prime Ministers came together in a meeting, Daniel was president of the council of Prime Ministers. Daniel's influence was so great that the king worshipped him.

Daniel 2:46: Then the king Nebuchadnezzar fell upon his face, and worshipped Daniel, and commanded that they should offer an oblation and sweet odours unto him.

As usual, Nebuchadnezzar was a figure head leader while every other thing in the land rose and fell on the orders of Daniel. As Daniel mounted a centre stage, he became the sole controller of the wealth of the Gentiles.

Just as God promoted Daniel, God will position you where you will control the wealth of the gentiles. The same God who brought Daniel out of captivity into prominence will place the wealth of the gentiles in your hands.

☞ Wealth Transfer And Israel

The children of Israel too experienced wealth transfer. Initially, Israel was poor and served the ungodly, but when wealth transfer took place, the riches of the Gentiles were given to the children of Israel.

Exodus 12:36: And the Lord gave the people favour in the sight of the Egyptians, so that they lent unto them such things as they required. And they spoiled the Egyptians.

One of the methods of wealth transfer is that, God can enrich His children at the expense of the ungodly. God blessed the nation of Israel several times in their history, by making them inherit instances of wealth transfer as recorded in 2 Chronicle 20. God made the Gentiles to lose precious materials and Israel acquired wealth at their expense.

One of these days, God will make you gather the spoils of the Gentiles. There is a prophecy which I must make clear to you at this moment. God is going to transfer the wealth of the wicked to his children. God gave us this prophecy during the watchnight service preceding 2005. That is why God's children need to be fully prepared to receive the gains of this transfer. God wants you to position yourself properly in order to benefit maximally from wealth transfer.

STEADY AND CONSISTENT

Children of God must be fully prepared and spiritually ready in order to receive and retain the gains which will accrue from wealth transfer. Your relationship with God must get to a top gear so that, when you receive the wealth you will not lose it.

No doubt you need wealth transfer. As a child of God who has a burden for evangelism, you cannot afford spending three hours in the kitchen trying to cook rice with a dilapidated stove. Poverty will hinder you from fulfilling your call or carrying out your obligations in the area of evangelism.

A church that is made up of poor and struggling members, will find it difficult to take the light of the gospel to a world pervaded by darkness.

It is not a sin for believers to be rich. Poverty or riches can never be a yard stick for going to hell or heaven. The poor man can go to hell fire while a rich man can go to heaven. It is not a crime to be rich, neither is there anything righteous about poverty. As a child of God you can have money, but don't ever allow money to have you.

You can control money without allowing it to control your life. As far as heaven is concerned every provision needed for your prosperity has been made. What we need today is aggressive prayer in the area of prosperity. As far as God is concerned, what it takes to make every believer prosper, has been made available.

The ball is now in your court. There is a great deal of wealth waiting for a transfer. You must arise and possess your possessions. Now is the time to be a beneficiary of wealth transfer. This is the season of possessing the riches of the gentiles. Pray, until an immeasurable amount of wealth is transferred from the coffers of the ungodly to yours.

THE BANE OF IGNORANCE

There is nothing that robs people of their blessings like ignorance. You cannot benefit maximally from an agenda that you are completely ignorant of. Financial abundance is your covenant right.

There are four major levels in life. Those who do not h ave at all, e.g. beggars. Those that have, but not enough. Those that have just enough. Those that have more than enough, i.e., overflowing.

These four levels are practical descriptions of levels of poverty and prosperity.

If you are a good student of the Bible, you would have discovered that poverty is a by-product of ignorance.

You cannot live above the level of information given to you. Progress, increase and prosperity are impossible without an inward change. An inward change takes place when you apply information to your situation. You require access to wealth in order to accomplish any tangible thing on earth.

Whatever you have acquired has cost you something. It is God's pleasure to bless His people. Our father, God, takes delight in seeing us blessed and living in prosperity. As such, God wants to give you an overflowing measure of blessings.

Abraham, for example, was abundantly blessed. Today we sing "Abraham's blessing are mine", simply because the blessings bestowed upon Abraham was so much that it is still flowing to us till date.

Members of the demonic kingdom know that, the

shortest route to the realm where human beings are controlled is the high way of riches. Therefore, they device many methods of enriching men and women. Thus, the greater bulks of the money in the world are in their coffers.

In most part of the world, the richest people are mostly unbelievers. I came across a magazine during one of my ministerial trips to England titled 'One Thousand Richest British People'. I became curious and purchased a copy. My intention was to find out if there was any believer listed among the whole lot. Unfortunately, I could not identify a single Christian in the list. It was indeed a great challenge. It lends credence to the fact that the children of darkness have indeed, captured the wealth of the world. But not to worry, they can go ahead and amass wealth, God will soon divert their riches to His children.

As God's children, we need to experience and benefit from God's wealth transfer agenda. In those days, believers were proud of their poverty. A lot of people accept poverty as a norm. Holiness and poverty were seen as virtues and as what believers must experience in order to get to heaven. But we now see that this is not true.

Decades ago, poverty was seen as a symbol of humility. I remember the church I attended when I was growing up. We lived in abject poverty while we attended that church. No member had a car. The highest vehicle owned by a member was a Raleigh bicycle.

However, a particular member broke the jinx and prospered through aggressive prayer. The name of the brother was Amos. He was the only Igbo speaking member of a Yoruba speaking church. Brother Amos did not understand whatever transpired during the service, the only thing he never joked about was the prayer session.

Whenever prayer points were given out in Yoruba language, he would quickly ask an enlightened member to interpret them in English language. Then, Brother Amos would pray violently. His voice would continue to ring out loud, even after the allotted time to the prayer was over.

To Brother Amos, prayer was a do or die affair. He would pray until his clothes were soaked with his sweat. He kept on praying until he had an unusual experience one night. He slept as usual and God woke him up early in the morning saying, "lift up your pillow and check what is under it." To his surprise he found a dead red headed lizard.

The Lord told Brother Amos, "the lizard was introduced into your life when you were a baby. It is the spirit of poverty, your wealth was stolen by a satanic agent who programmed the lizard into your life. Your wealth has been restored to you. I have decided to show you the lizard so that you can appreciate what I have done for you and be able to praise Me." That was the end of poverty for brother Amos.

Doors of prosperity were thrown wide open for Brother Amos. Within one week he was able to buy a Mercedes Benz car. By the following Sunday, Brother Amos brought his car to the church. That was the first time a member of our church parked a car outside the building. It was such a new experience that members found it difficult to co ncentrate on the sermon t hat day. This happened because Brother Amos recovered his stolen riches. At this point I want you to close your eyes and pray saying:

Every wealth stolen from me when I was young, I repossess you by fire, in Jesus' name.

THE SATANIC STRATEGY

As a result of his resolve to control the wealth that is available in the world, satan has d eviced ma ny desperate and ungodly methods of obtaining money. These methods pro mise ac quiring money witho ut putting in any serious effort.

We shall examine those methods to avoid falling into the trap carefully concealed by the enemy.

☞ **Lying**

A lot of people tell lies in o rder to acquire wealth. Most of the worldly business methods e ntail telling lies. A lot of people can lie insisting that what they are saying is the truth and nothing but the truth.

☞ **Use Of Charms Or Voodoo**

A lot of fetish priests have produced charms that are supposedly capable of making people rich. The devil has so endowed fetish priests with power as to make them produce wealth, through ritual sacrifices.

☞ Cheating

The devil has designed clever methods of cheating and obtaining money by false pretence. People now cheat colleagues, business partners and even family members just to control wealth.

☞ Stealing

This is another method designed by the devil to make people get rich illegally. People steal, using diverse methods, today. There are people who falsify accounts in the office, perpetrate fraud on the internet and involve themselves in fraud.

☞ Prophetic Charismatic Manipulation Of People

A lot of people are being manipulated through fake prophecies. There are too many commercial prophets today, who are using the spirit of divination to deceive.

☞ Fake Products

A lot of fake products are on sale in the market. People resort to selling fake items just to make quick money. A friend of mine once bought a tin of Bournvita, but when he opened it, it was filled with sand.

☞ Deception

Deception is the order of the day in the business world today.

☞ Armed Robbery

This is another satanic method devised for acquiring money illegally. The number of robbery cases is increasing and many innocent lives have been terminated before or after being robbed of their goods.

☞ Manipulation

A lot of people use the weapon of manipulation in order to become rich. People have made up their minds that they will get rich through any conceivable method of manipulation.

☞ Prostitution

The act of prostitution has been perfected by both young and older ladies. Besides the professional prostitutes who litter the streets, there a re executive prostitutes who live in their own homes, ac ademic prostitutes as well as teenage prostitutes who secretly engage in the cursed practice.

☞ Gambling

Gambling is one of the means devised by the devil to deceive many people and send them to hell fire. Today, governments and organised companies are involved in gambling. Gambling has assumed a prominent place on the internet. The lure of making quick money has pushed many people to gambling.

☞ Falsification

A lot of people go about in search of jobs with forged certificates. Many people find it easier to buy their admissionrather than work for it. A lo t of people buy fake foreign degrees just to make money or get wealth illegally.

☞ **Pulling Down Others In Order To Get To The Top**

Today, many people are ready to pull down their fellow workers just to gain financial advantage and promotion.

☞ **Inflating Prices Of Commodities**

This is the trend in our society today. Business people and traders inflate prices of commodities in order to make excessive gain and get rich quickly.

☞ **Stealing Of People's Virtues Through Diabolical Means**

Whenever children of darkness discover that a particular person has great virtues or when they come across those who are destined to become rich, they consult fetish priests or occult masters with an eye of stealing the virtues of potentially prosperous people.

☞ **Hoarding Materials**

Business men and women as well as traders hoard goods in order to create artificial scarcity. As soon as scarcity is created, they offer the same goods for sale at exorbitant prices.

☞ Over Invoicing

Many people who are in business get involved in lots of sharp practices. They often increase the real value of goods by writing false invoices. Their intention generally is to make more money.

☞ Transfer Of Birthright

In some families, the birthright of some people have been transferred to others just to make them inherit or acquire riches of others.

☞ Brain Exchange

People are ready to do anything in order to get rich illegally. When people discovered that there are people with exceptional intelligence they go ahead to exchange such brains for that of those who are dull. The purpose here, is to get rich through falsehood.

☞ Elimination Of Competitors

A lot of people send hired killers to those who are competing with them or business associates who stand in their way. Others eliminate those who do not allow them to beco me rich by ge tting rid of them through remotely controlled charms.

You may wonder why the enemy has created these channels of amassing wealth illegally. It is simply because satan wants to control human life by controlling wealth. The devil has placed his focus on those who have access to money. He knows that to allow money to get to t he hands of the righteous, is to allow the saints to depopulate his kingdom by investing their wealth on evangelism.

We must turn the tide to our favour. We must pray and command the enemy to vomit all the wealthhe has swallowed.

ARROWS OF WEALTH DESTRUCTION

The devil is ready to do anything in order to obtain wealth and use it illegally. If the enemy cannot succeed in transferring wealth, he will steal it. If he cannot steal it he will plan to destroy it. When the devil knows you have decided to avoid his wealth traps, he will attack you so that you can remain poor. The enemy does this by using the arrow of wealth destruction. Unfortunately, these arrows have entered into the lives, bodies and destinies of believers. We need to pray until these arrows jump out and their poison are neutralized.

EVIL ARROWS

Below are the methods the devil uses in order to steal or transfer the wealth of God's children.

☞ **Debts**

Debt has been used by the devil to keep you perpetually poor. The devil will instigate someone to start with a little debt. He will cajole the fellow to add a little more debt. At the end of the day, battling with huge debt will keep the victim perpetually poor. If you are a victim of the arrow of debts. You must pray until indebtedness becomes a thing of the past.

☞ **Wrong Investments**

Wrong investment is one weapon the devil uses to steal people's wealth When you invest huge amounts of money on an enterprise and the whole money goes down the drain, you may not be able to know what it means to experience prosperity No matter what efforts you make, wrong investments will keep you miles away from wealth.

☞ Failure At The Edge Of Breakthrough

This is one poisonous arrow which the enemy uses. The devil programmes ·fàlure and activates it at the point when people are at the edge of breakthroughs. He will allow people to see wealth afar but he will not allow them to possess their divinely given wealth.

☞ Profit Starvation

The devil will allow people to do business but he will ensure that he starves them of anything called profit through diabolical means. This is how he makes people to labour as elephants and eat like ants.

☞ Poor Patronage

Whenever the devil steals or destroys people's wealth, he orchestrates poor patronage. If a believer sells goods and patronage is low, wealth will become elusive.

☞ Witchcraft Hanging

The devil, through the instrumentality of witches,

hangs the money or wealth which his victims are supposed to acquire. As long as wealth remains hanging, the victim will not be able to handle real wealth throughout his entire life time.

☞ **Satanic Business Partners**

The devil has robbed people of their wealth by programming satanic business partners into their lives. When a believer teams up with a satanic business partner, there will be great loses. The demonic partner will be paying his tithes to fetish priests while the believer will take his tithes to the church. The business venture will be contaminated through the former's practise. For the believer, wealth will be elusive.

Again the Bible tells us that the wicked is under a curse. The word of God declares. "Say to the wicked that it shall be ill with him." You cannot bless someone whom God had cursed. If you try to do so you will also come under a curse.

☞ **Evasion of Tithe**

A lot of people evade tithes today. As God blesses

them, they do everything to avoid paying their tithes. Some people manage to pay their tithes once in a while. While others are perpetual offenders. Such people are taking the key and shutting the windows of heaven. Such people avoid paying their tithes because they feel the amount is too high.

Is any amount too big to pay as tithe? Why pray for breakthroughs, when you know that the size of the breakthroughs will be so big that you wil l not be able to pay your tithes.

You must pay your tithes even if the amount appears big. Don't play games with God. Be faithful. God requires only a tenth of your profit or income. If you ever decide to rob God by taking that which belongs to God and adding it to your own, you may never experience prosperity. You will only end up inviting the devil to come and steal your wealth.

Malachi 3:8-10: Will a man rob God? Yet ye have robbed me. But ye say, Wherein have we robbed thee? In tithes and offerings. Ye are cursed with a curse: for ye have robbed me, even this whole nation. Bring ye all the tithes into the storehouse, that there may be meat in mine house, and prove me now herewith, saith the Lord of hosts, if I will not open you the windows of heaven, and pour you out a blessing, that there shall not be room enough to receive it.

Some people run to deliverance centres when they experience financial insufficiency. Such people do not really need deliverance. What they need is repentance and obedience. How can a believer own a company without paying his tithes? How can a believer expect God to prosper him with incomplete tithes?

When you fail to pay your tithes you are inviting the arrows of the devourer and wealth destruction.

☞ Leaky Pocket

This is one of the most poisonous arrows of wealth destruction. The devil programmes leaky pockets into the lives of many people. As they labour to fill their pocket, the devil labours to empty it. Then the Bible says:

Haggai 1:5-7 : Now therefore thus saith the Lord of hosts; Consider your ways. Ye have sown much, and bring in little; ye eat, but ye have not enough; ye drink, but ye are not filled with drink; ye clothe you, but there is none warm; and he that earneth wages earneth wages to put it into a bag with holes.

Thus saith the Lord of hosts; Consider your ways.

You must pray and ask God to block every avenue of leakage in your finances.

☞ **Sponsoring Abortion**

Those who sp onsor abortion in wha tever form will receive arrows of wealth destruction. If your money is used to destroy lives, the devil will ensure that your finances are destroyed. Unknown to most pe ople, this is a satanic strategy for wealth destruction.

☞ **Gambling**

A lot of people lose huge financial resources through gambling.

☞ **Alcoholism**

This is an avenue for draining finances. Alcoholics are always extremely poor. Even when the rich man begins to receive the arrow of alc oholism, his riches will soon go down the drain.

☞ **Bribery**

This is another arrow of wealth destruction. Bribery is an ungodly practice. When you g ive bribes, you may

-73-

get results but such results will be cancelled sooner or later by the evil consequences of bribery. You may make money now and lose it later. At the end of the day the entire project will be unprofitable.

☞ **Wrong Attitude To Money**

Whenever the devil wants to attack you with the arrow of wealth destruction, he will programme wrong attitude to money into your life. He will either programme careless attitude towards making good money or, love for filthy lucre into your life. Once your attitude is wrong, your wealth will be destroyed.

☞ **Laziness**

This is one weapon which the enemy uses when he wants to fire the arrow of wealth destruction at his victim. Even if a lazy man inherits money, the wealth will diminish with the passage of time. Remember, the Bible says

Proverbs 6:9-11: How long wilt thou sleep, O sluggard? when wilt thou arise out of thy sleep? Yet a little sleep, a little slumber, a little folding of the hands to sleep: So shall thy poverty come as one that travelleth, and thy want as an armed man.

☞ **Vagabond Spirit**

A vagabond can be described as a rolling stone which gathers no moss. A vagabond will go from place to place rather than address himself to profitable hardwork.

☞ **Strange Money**

There are lots of strange money in circulation. Wealth begins to disappear when it mixes with strange money.

☞ **Arrows Of Infirmities**

When a rich man becomes sick mysteriously, he will keep on spending money until his entire wealth is frittered away.

☞ **Territorial Bondage**

There are territorial powers in charge of environments or communities. If you operate your business in an environment where territorial powers are averse to business success, your business may not prosper.

☞ **Evil Transfer Of Blessing, Satanic**

Relocation Of Wealth, Placing Wealth In Wrong Hands

When demonic powers transfer blessings, wealth is destroyed. If the devil relocates wealth, he will tamper with the wealth which God has allocated to you. This is one of the high points of satanic agenda. The devil will do everything to take wealth away from good hands and place it in wrong hands.

☞ **Wandering Stars**

A star may be endowed with uncommon glory, but when it wanders from one place to another, the shine and the glory disappears.

☞ **Activities Of Devourers**

A lot of brilliant and hard-working people are poor due to the activities of devourers. The duty of demonic wealth devourers is to ensure that wealth is completely wasted.

☞ **Get-Rich-Quick Syndrome**

Those who have been lured into the trap of get-rich-quick programmes, have discovered that the more they looked the less they saw. Tho se who are so much in a hurry to get rich, end up hurting themselves. Don't forget the words of the Scripture.

1 Tim. 6:9-10: But they that will be rich fall into temptation and a snare, and into many foolish and hurtful lusts, which drown men in destruction and perdition. For the love of money is the root of all evil: which while some coveted after, they have erred from the faith, a nd pierced themselves through with many sorrows.

You must not allow any of those arrows of wealth destruction to prosper in your life. Just as the devil has vowed to fire his arrows and tamper with wealth, you must refuse to be one of the victims.

THE WEALTH TRANSFER STRATEGY

Members of the dark kingdom have over the years, perfected the act of t ransferring wealth and virtue. They make use of the weapon of spiritual summoning, illegal transfer and demonic theft to short-change and rob their victims. As t hese s atanic agents continue to pe rpetrate various degrees of evil,

God is also raising up His children and empowering us to produce and multiply wealth.

In Bible days, there were many instances where there was godly production and multiplication of wealth. This goes to tell us that members of satanic kingdom can device means of acquiring wealth. Children of God can also acquire wealth through the power of God.

Let us go through a few examples. Jesus fed five thousand people miraculously. He produced wine from water. He also put money in the mouth of a fish. By the power of God, Elijah multiplied the seeds of the widow. Elisha also performed a similar miracle.

In contemporary times, the great Apostle Joseph Ayo Babalola owned several buildings. God blessed him with the houses miraculously. He bought the houses for peanuts when the owners abandoned them because they were bewitched.

In those days, some people were forced out of their homes after they had spent a large amount of money building the houses. There were instances of loud noises, shrieks and crying. Ther e were also so unds of footsteps and pounding on the roofs by unseen forces. The owners of the houses noticed sounds of movement without seeing anyone or anything. These haunted buildings made many owners to run away from their houses. Some of them approached Apostle Babalola, begging him to buy the buildings for a ridiculously small amount of money.

The Apostle later became popular as a man who could buy any haunted building. Thus, the unbelievers were busy selling them for almost nothing and t hat was how he owned several houses which he never built. This is what we refer to as wealth transfer.

I almost had a s imilar experience some years ago. The only thing was that I did not have enough money then to acquire a building that was haunted. The building was a fantastic e difice but the owner could not live in it. He told us that there were strange voices every night.

A few pastors accompanied me to pray and a noint the place. As soon as we got there we began to hear the same sound which the owner of the building complained about. A violent sound came from the direction of the roof. We asked for his permission to break the asbestos ceiling a little bit. As soon as we ripped the ceiling open with a big stick, we splashed anointing oil into the roof. There was a loud bang as a mighty python hit the floor. Everyone, including me took to our heels.

We managed to get back to the site of the building and peeped into it. To our surprise, we found five live pythons on the floor. Since we knew that we were involved in spiritual warfare, we decided to fight the pythons spiritually. We kept on splashing anointing oil on them. The more we did, the weaker the pythons became. When it became obvious that the pythons were no longer harmful we went ahead to hit the pythons with sticks till they all died. We went into a session of praise worship after we had succeeded in killing the demonic pythons. At the end, we picked up our Bibles and started to go away.

To our surprise, the man followed us saying "I am sorry, I can no longer live in this building. I know that the serpents are all dead but I'm still scared. The idea of ever having five mighty pythons in m y ceil ing will continue to haunt me. Is there anything you can do?"

If it were to be now, we would have offered to buy the house. That was an opportunity to have experienced wealth transfer. The man eventua lly sold the house off at a very ridiculous amount.

A man once bought three buses. The three buses were involved in accidents mysteriously. The owner of the buses got tired knowing that a spell had been cast upon the buses. He decided to get ri d of the buses and approached a Christian brother.

Again, the price was unbelievably low. The person who bought the buses being a believer who was familiar with spiritual warfare and deliverance seized the opportunity as an avenue for wealth transfer.

Our father God owns h eaven and earth. We cannot afford to live as paupers when our father is the originator of wealth. T o benefit from the wealth transfer agenda, we need a fresh understanding of wealth transfer strategy. What then is the strategy for wealth transfer?

Find below the divine blue print for wealth transfer:

☞ Seek Yea First The kingdom Of God

We alth without salvation amounts to poverty. If you have all the money in this world and you have not known Christ, you are the poorest man in t he history of the world. A lot of people are busy seeking wealth when they should be busy seeking t he kingdom of God. All the wealth in t his world put together are no t worth the value of a single soul. The Bible says:

Mark 8: 36 : For what shall it profit a man, if he shall gain the whole world, and lose his own soul?

There is no profit in any thing else except in see king the face of God. When you seek God's kingdom, you will find God as well as true riches. God has promised to endow those who seek His face with divine blessings and riches. The Bible terms riches as "all other things" whic h shall be added to the true seeker.

Matthew 6:33: But seek ye first the kingdom of God, and his righteousness; and all these things shall be added unto you.

You must do everything you can to ensure that you

are born-again and that your name is in the Book of Life. You must remain in Go d's kingdom if you want to retain your wealth. If you have wealth and you are not making use of it as a child of God, such misuse of wealth will provoke divine withdrawal. At the end of the day, the wealth may be transferred to unbelievers as a form of punishment.

☞ **You Must Live A Holy Life**

Your life must be clean enough for God to trust you. When you are holy within or without, there is no amount of wealth which God cannot transfer to you. The fact that you share in God's nature of holiness will propel Him to make you a tr ustee or a t reasurer who can handle wealth on His behalf.

☞ **You Must Attack The Gates Of Hell**

The primary function of the gate of hell is to send people away from the place of their blessings. They provoke their victims and drive them away from the corridors of divine favour. They do not want anyone to prosper. Their wicked ac tivities en ter on wasting people's wealth and causing failure at the edge of breakthroughs. You must de al with the ga tes of hell today.

☞ Get Spiritual Information Concerning What You Must Do In Order To Receive Divine Wealth

Seek specific spiritual guidance before you start any business venture. Don't jump into any business just because others are making it. Let God show you the secrets of making it and succeeding with a business idea before commencement.

☞ Pray To Discover Your Destiny

Discover what you have been divinely destined to do. Your destiny will be fulfilled only when you discover what God created you to be or do in life. When God has destined you to succeed by doing a particular line of business, you will achieve success with ease. You will not need to struggle as everything will fall in line.

If you are pursuing a business agenda other than the one God has destined you to pursue, you may end up chasing shadows. Discover your destiny and pursue it.

☞ Change Your Giving Patterns, Sow Seeds

Sacrificially

Tithes and offerings are an insurance against poverty. Each tithe or offering you give has a voice. It will speak prosperity and wealth. Remember it was Abel's offering that spoke to God. Cain's offering also spoke to God. Your offering has the ability to speak.

There was a time in the Bible when David had a problem with God and God started to destroy the people. A prophet taught David what to do to stop the tragedy. He told David to offer a definite sacrificial offering unto God.

Sacrificial giving will always provoke divine blessings. Don't eat your seeds. Unless you sow seeds there will be no harvest. If you want to unlock your finances, give sacrificially. God cannot multiply anything, unless you give him something.

The farmer who sows no seed will harvest nothing. Most of the time, God will ask you to give your best in order to receive His best. You must be a tither, no matter how small your income is. Members and ministers who fail to pay their tithes will remain under attack.

Prosperity is impossible without sowing a seed. You must be a giver if you want to unlock your finances. Prosperity can only respond to the voice of the seed sown by you.

One of the secrets of prosperity is the act of sowing seeds. You must exercise some restraints when you are giving to God. Avoid any form of showman ship. If you pay your tithes in the manner prescribed by the word of God, there will be great blessings.

Don't refrain from giving your tithes and offering. Don't ever come up with the idea of borrowing your tithes. That will amount to stealing. You may decide to solve temporary problems by spending your tithes. But you will create more problems for yourself.

Eve desired a knowledge which she did not need. God gave her a garden, but she went after the tree. God drove her and her man out of the garden. If God asks you to pay your tithe and you refuse, God will withdraw His wealth. Many believers need to repent of failure to pay their tithes.

☞ **Engage In P rophetic P raying F or Fi nancial Breakthr ough**

There is a world of difference between general praying and prophetic praying. Prophetic praying will always produce exceptional results.

You can get involved with prophetic pray ing through the following methods!

a. *Call forth those things which be not as though they are. This kind of praying will always bring something out of nothing.*

b. *Pray poverty destroying prayers.*

c. *Pray wealth releasing prayers.*

d. *Pray poverty into the camp of the enemy.*

e. *Draw virtues from the camp of the enemy.*

f. *Remove the robes of their rich men.*

g. *Capture the enemy's staff of bread.*

h. *Sentence the servants to trekking .*

i. *Pray them down from riding horses.*

j.   *Pray your prince back to riding on horses.*

k.   *Pray wealth transfer prayers.*

You need to pray these kinds of prayers if you want to experience prosperity.

☞ **Work Hard**

There is no room for laziness in the kingdom of God.

☞ **Identify The Enemy Of Prosperity And Avoid Them**

Keep the enemy of prosperity at arms length.

☞ **Invest Wisely**

Whenever you want to invest , be prayerful and wise.

☞ **Try As Much As You Can To Avoid Be ing Either A Debtor Or A Borrower**

Debt is a destroyer, avoid it. Don't allow debts to truncate your destiny. The enemy hat es to see us prosper. Whenever the devil knows that God intend s to raise you up as someone who will channel His wealth towards the needs of t he gospel, the devil will attack you.

I went through a lot of battles when I was young because, the devil knew my future. I almost lost my life when I was about sitting for the School Certificate Examination. I was just passing by when a neighbour called my name saying; "Come and help us remove this frying pan from the stove."

I never knew what the devil had in stock for me. I was not sleeping, I was fully awake, I was simply watching the frying pan from a distance. Suddenly, the oil in the frying pan suddenly became a ball of fire and landed on my legs. I was transfixed to the spot where I was. My leg began to roast like chicken being fried in hot oil.

Unfortunately the three men that were around who could have rescued me were arguing about the best first aid methods to apply.

The first man prescribed iced-water, the second man prescribed raw eggs while the third man prescribed a raw cornstarch. They never could come to a common decision.

The more they lingered, the worse my condition

became. My leg was badly roasted. Eventually, when they decided, they chose the wrong medication of the three; iced-water. My leg got so bad that I could no longer put on shoes. I had a shoe on one leg while the second was bare. That was how I was going to school while getting ready for my examination.

One day soon afterwards, one of the teachers gave a group of students including me, a hot chase and I got wounded in the process. I ended up with a fractured arm. With a bad leg and a bad hand, I was compelled to pray when I discovered that it would be impossible to write my examination. That was when God spoke to me saying. "Son, if you do not pray and go into warfare, your enemies will get rid of you."

At that point I declared war against the enemies of my progress. God gave me victory. Now I know that the enemy was after my progress and prosperity.

Unless you get serious with spiritual warfare, you may never possess your possession. You must go into warfare and pray until power changes hands. Pray in order to benefit from the wealth transfer agenda today.

Prayer Points

1 Oh heavens over my prosperity, open by fire in the name of Jesus

2 Angels of poverty, clear from the gate of my breakthroughs in the name of Jesus.

3 Oh wealth jump out of the abdication of the wicked and locate me now in the name of Jesus.

4 You children of darkness continue to labour, at the end of your labour transfer the wealth to me in the name of Jesus.

5 I eat the sweat of my enemies by the power in the blood of Jesus in the name of Jesus.

6 Angels of the living God, pursue wealth into my hands in the name of Jesus.

7 Any power that wants me to die as a pauper, you are a liar, die in the name of Jesus.

8 I withdraw my wealth from the hand of the bondwoman and her children, i n th e name of Jesus.

9 I will not squander my divine opportunities, in the name of Jesus.

10 I dismantle any power working against my efficiency, in the name of Jesus.

11 I refuse to lock the door of blessings against myself, in the name of Jesus.

12 I refuse to be a wandering star, in the name of Jesus.

13 I refuse to appear to disappear, in the name of Jesus.

14 Let the riches of the Gentiles be transferred to me, in the name of Jesus.

15 Let the angels of the Lord pursue every enemy of my prosperity to destruction, in the name of Jesus.

16 Let the sword of the Goliathof poverty turn against it, in the name of Jesus.

17 Let wealth change h ands in my life, in the name of Jesus.

18 O Lord, make a hole in the roof for me for my prosperity.

19 Let the yoke of poverty upon my li fe be dashed to pieces, in the name of Jesus.

20 Let every satanic siren scaring away my helpers be

silenced, in the name of Jesus.

21 Let every masquerading power swallowing my prosperity be destroyed, in the name of Jesus.

22 Let every coffin constructed against my prosperity swallow the owner, in the name of Jesus.

23 Let the ways of the angels of poverty delegated against me be dark and slippery, in the name of Jesus.

24 Lord Jesus, hold my purse.

25 Every demonic scarcity, be dissolved by fire, in the name of Jesus.

26 By the wealthy name of Jesus, let heavenly resources rush to my door.

27 I attack my lack with the sword of fire, in the name of Jesus.

28 Satanic debt and credit, be dissolved, in the name of Jesus.

29 Oh Lord, be my eternal cashier.

30 I bind the spirit of debt. I shall not borrow to eat, in the name of Jesus.

31 Every evil meeting summoned against my

prosperity, scatter without repair, in the name of Jesus.

32 Every arrow of wickedness, fired against my prosperity, be disgraced, in the name of Jesus.

33 Let my life magnetize favour for breakthroughs, in the name of Jesus.

34 I arrest every gadget of poverty, in the name of Jesus.

35 I recover my blessings from any body of water, forest and satanic banks, in the name of Jesus.

36 Let all my departed glory be restored, in the name of Jesus.

37 Let all my departed virtues be restored, in the name of Jesus.

38 Let God arise and let all my stubborn pursuers scatter, in the name of Jesus.

39 Every attack by evil night creatures, be disgraced, in the name of Jesus.

40 Let the wings of every spirit flying against me be dashed to pieces, in the name of Jesus.

41 Angels of the living God, search the land of the

living and the land of the dead and recover my stolen properties, in the name of Jesus.

42 Every gadget of frustration, be dashed to pieces, in the name of Jesus.

43 I break every curse of poverty working upon my life, in the name of Jesus.

44 I bind every spirit drinking the blood of my prosperity, in the name of Jesus.

45 O Lord, create new and profitable opportunities for me.

46 Let ministry angels bring customers and favour to me, in the name of Jesus.

47 Anyone occupying my seat of prosperity, clear away, in the name of Jesus.

48 Lord, make a way for me in the land of the living.

49 I bind the spirit of fake and useless investment, in the name of Jesus.

50 All unsold materials, be sold with profit, in the name of Jesus.

51 Let all business failure be converted to success, in the name of Jesus.

52 Every curse on my hands and legs, be broken, in the name of Jesus.

53 O Lord, embarrass me with abundance in every area of my life.

54 Every strange money affecting my pro sperity, be neutralized, in the name of Jesus.

55 Let brassy heavens break forth and bring rain, in the name of Jesus.

56 I break the cont rol of every spirit of poverty over my life, in the name of Jesus.

57 Lord Jesus, anoint my eyes to see the hidden riches of this world.

58 Lord Jesus, advertise Your breakthroughs in my life.

59 Let the riches of the ungodly be transferred into my hands, in the name of Jesus.

60 I will rise above the unbelievers around me, in the name of Jesus.

61 O Lord, make me a reference point of divine blessings.

62 Let blessings invade my life, in the name of Jesus.

63 Let the anointing of excellence fall on me , in the name of Jesus.

64 I disarm satan king and authority over my prosperity, in the name of Jesus.

65 Let harvest meet harvest in my life, in the name of Jesus.

66 Let harvest overtake the sower in my life, in the name of Jesus.

67 Every curse pronounced against my source of income, be broken, in the name of Jesus.

68 Let my breakthroughs turn around for good, in t he name of Jesus.

69 Curses working against my destiny, break, in the name of Jesus.

70 O Lord, network me with divine helpers.

71 Let life-transforming breakthroughs overtake me, in the name of Jesus.

72 Let divine ability overtake me, in the name of Jesus.

73 O Lord, lead me to those who will bless me.

74 Let my favour frustrate the plant of the enemy, in

the name of Jesus.

75 I will witness the downfalls of my strongman, in the name of Jesus.

76 I will be a lender and not a borrower, in the name of Jesus.

77 My labour shall not be in vain, in the name of Jesus.

78 Let the blessings which there will be no room to receive overtake me, in the name of Jesus.

79 O Lord, plant me by the rivers of prosperity.

80 Unknown evil seeds in my life, I command you to refuse to germinate, in the name of Jesus.

81 I refuse to get stuck on one level of blessing, in the name of Jesus.

82 I shall possess all the good things I pursue, in the name of Jesus.

83 Every effect of cursed house and land upon my prosperity, break, in the name of Jesus.

84 I shall possess all the good things I pursue, in the name of Jesus.

85 Every effect of cursed house and land upon my

prosperity, break, in the name of Jesus.

86 Every power shielding me away from breakthroughs, fall down and die, in the name of Jesus.

87 Let the garden of my life yield super abundance, in the name of Jesus.

88 Every desert spirit, loose hold upon my life, in the name of Jesus.

89 Holy Spirit, plug my life into divineprosperity, in the name of Jesus.

90 Every Achan in the camp of my breakthroughs, be exposed and be disgraced, in the name of Jesus.

91 Every power operating demonic gadget against my prosperity,fall down and die, in the name of Jesus.

92 Every power passing evil current into my finances, lose your hold, in the name of Jesus.

93 I break every cycle of financial turbulence, in the name of Jesus.

94 I smash the head of poverty, walk out of my life now, in the name of Jesus.

95 Ugly feet of poverty, walk out of my life now, in

the name of Jesus.

96 Let every garment of poverty received the fire of God. in the name of Jesus.

97 I reject financial burial, in the name of Jesus.

98 Let every garment of poverty received the fire of God. in the name of Jesus.

99 I reject financial burial, in the name of Jesus.

100 I reject every witchcraft burial, in the name of Jesus.

101 Woe unto every vessels of poverty pursuing me, in the name of Jesus.

102 Let the fire of God burn away evil spiritual properties, in the name of Jesus.

103 Poverty-identification marks, be rubbed off by the blood of Jesus.

104 O Lord, heal every financial leprosy in my life.

105 Let my foundation be strengthened to carry divine prosperity, in the name of Jesus.

106 Every stolen and satanically transferre d virtues, be restored, in the name of Jesus.

107 Let every ordination of debt over my life be canceled, in the name of Jesus.

108 O Lord, create newer and profitable opportunities for me.

109 Every strange fire ignited against my prosperity, be quenched, in the name of Jesus.

110 Let those sending my money to spiritual mortuary fall down and die, in the name of Jesus.

111 Every power scaring away my prosperity, be paralysed, in the name of Jesus.

112 Every familiar spirit sharing my money before I received it, be bound permanently, in the name of Jesus.

113 Let every inherited design of poverty melt away by fire, in the name of Jesus.

114 Let every evil re-arrangement of prosperity be dismantled, in the name of Jesus.

115 Lead me, O Lord, to my own hand that flows with milk and honey.

116 Let satanic giants occupying my promised land fall down and die, in the name of Jesus.

117 O Lord, empower me t o climb my mountain o f prosperity.

118 Strongman of poverty in m y life, fall down and die, in the name of Jesus.

119 Spirits of famine and hunger my life is not your candidate, in the name of Jesus.

120 I remove my name from the book of financial embarrassment, in the name of Jesus.

121 Every power reinforcing poverty against me, loose your hold, in the name of Jesus.

122 I release myself from every bondage of poverty, in the name of Jesus.

123 The riches of the gentiles shall come to me, in the name of Jesus.

124 Let divine magnet of prosperity be planted in my hands, in the name of Jesus.

125 I retrieve my purse from the hand of Judas, in the name of Jesus.

126 Let there be a reverse trans fer of my satanically transferred wealth, in the name of Jesus.

127 I take over the wealth of the sinner, in the name

of Jesus.

128 I recover the steering wheels of my wealth from the hand of evil drivers, in the name of Jesus.

129 I refuse to lock the door of blessings against myself, in the name of Jesus.

130 O Lord, revive my blessings.

131 O Lord, return my stolen blessings.

132 O Lord, sends God's angels to bring me blessings.

133 O Lord, let everything that needs change in my life to bring me blessings be changed.

134 O Lord, uncover to me my key for prosperity.

135 Every power sitting on my wealth, fall down and die, in the name of Jesus.

136 O Lord, transfer the wealth of Laban to my Jacob.

137 Let all those who hate my prosperity be put to shame, in the name of Jesus.

138 Every evil bird swallowing my money, fall down and die, in the name of Jesus.

139 Every arrow of poverty, go back to where you came from, in the name of Jesus.

140 I bind every word spoken against my breakthroughs, in the name of Jesus.

141 Every business house energized by satan, fold up, in the name of Jesus.

142 I destroy every clock and timetable of poverty, in the name of Jesus.

143 Every water spirit, touch not my prosperity, in the name of Jesus.

144 Let men and women rush wealth to my doors, in the name of Jesus.

145 I reject temporary blessings, in the name of Jesus.

146 Every arrow of poverty energized by polygamy, fall down and die, in the name of Jesus.

147 Every arrow of poverty energized by household wickedness, fall down and die, in the name of Jesus.

148 Let power change hands in my finances, in the name of Jesus.

149 Let every serpent and scorpion of poverty die, in the name of Jesus.

150 I refuse to eat the bread of sorrow. I reject the

water of affliction, in the name of Jesus.

151 Let divine explosion fall upon my breakthroughs, in the name of Jesus.

152 The enemy will not drag my finances on the ground, in the name of Jesus.

153 O Lord, advertize Your wealth and power in my life, in the name of Jesus.

154 Let promotion meet promotion in my life, in the name of Jesus.

155 I pursue and overtake my enemies and recover my wealth from them, in the name of Jesus.

156 Holy Spirit, direct my hands into prosperity, in the name of Jesus.

157 Begin to thank God for answers to your prayers.

ALL OBTAINABLE AT:

- 322, Herbert Macaulay Way, Yaba, P.O. Box 12272, Ikeja, Lagos.

- MFM International Bookshop, 13, Olasimbo Street, Onike, Yaba, Lagos.

- All MFM Church branches nationwide and Christian bookstores.

Wealth Transfer Agenda

The Wealth Transfer Agenda is written with uncommon insight, practical attention to details, powerful scriptural exposition and rare prophetic perception. These have made the book a classic in every sense of the word.

In keeping with the divine programme which centres on making wealth to change hands from the camp of the ungodly to the camp of the righteous, The Wealth Transfer Agenda unveils deep mysteries on wealth. It details prophetic guidelines which if acted upon will turn a pauper to a prince and those living in penury to specimens of divine abundance and prosperity.

With this book in your hands you are going to experience unprecedented prosperity which will re-write your entire history.

About the Author

Dr. D. K. Olukoya is the General Overseer of the Mountain of Fire and Miracles Ministries and The Battle Cry Christian Ministries.

The Mountain of Fire and Miracles Ministries' Headquarters is the largest single Christian congregation in Africa with attendance of over 120,000 in single meetings.

MFM is a full gospel ministry devoted to the revival of Apostolic signs, Holy Ghost Fireworks, miracles and the unlimited demonstration of the power of God to deliver to the uttermost. Absolute holiness within and without as spiritual insecticide and pre-requisite for heaven is openly taught. MFM is a do-it-yourself Gospel Ministry, where your hands are trained to wage war and your fingers to do battle.

Dr. Olukoya holds a first class honours degree in Micro-biology from the University of Lagos and a PhD in Molecular Genetics from the University of Reading, United Kingdom. As a researcher, he has over seventy scientific publications to his credit.

Anointed by God, Dr. Olukoya is a prophet, evangelist, teacher and preacher of the Word. His life and that of his wife, Shade and their son Elijah Toluwani are living proofs that all power belongs to God.

ISBN -978-38083-1-1

84357019R00063

Made in the USA
Columbia, SC
15 December 2017